Your Book of Pressed and Dried Flowers

The *Your Book* Series

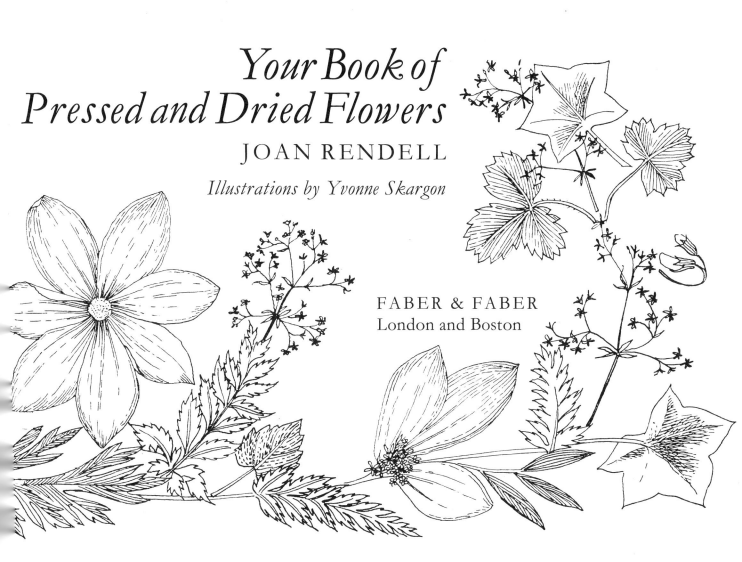

Your Book of
Pressed and Dried Flowers

JOAN RENDELL

Illustrations by Yvonne Skargon

FABER & FABER
London and Boston

First published in 1978 by
Faber and Faber Limited
3 Queen Square London WC1
Filmset and printed in Great Britain by
BAS Printers Limited, Over Wallop, Hampshire

British Library Cataloguing in Publication Data

Rendell, Joan
　　Your book of pressed and dried flowers.
　　1. Flowers – Collection and preservation –
　　Juvenile literature
　　I. Title
　　745.92　　　　　SB447

ISBN 0–571–11249–8

Contents

Illustrations

1 *How to use preserved plant material*

Most people like flowers and regret that they wither and fade so quickly. But flowers can be made to retain their beauty for very long periods, and there are various methods of preserving them.

When we talk about preserved flowers we usually think of two things – drying, and pressing blooms and foliage. In the one case flowers or leaves are preserved by being pressed under weights (perhaps just a heavy book) and in the other by being hung up to dry.

People have long been interested in the preserving of flowers and fragrances. The desert dwellers of Biblical times often placed bags of aromatic herbs between bedding and garments to keep them sweet-smelling, and the making of pot pourri (drying flower petals, small whole flowers and some leaves for their perfume) really began in earnest in Elizabethan times, when bunches of sweet-smelling flowers were hung to dry in rooms set aside for the purpose of making various forms of pot pourri. A book of recipes for pot pourri was published in 1682.

The Victorians were very enthusiastic about what they called 'drawing room crafts'. These were crafts which they could learn without any special tuition, which they could practise in their homes and which provided them with a pleasant hobby. The pressing of plant material was a favourite pastime with them and they did not confine themselves to gathering flowers and leaves; they also pressed seaweed and made fascinating pictures with it. In fact, seaweed was the first plant material to be used for pictures; it was after becoming proficient in making seaweed pictures that the Victorians turned their attention to flower pictures, which are still made today. Queen Victoria was fourteen years old when she mounted pressed seaweeds in an album and gave them to her friend the young Queen of Portugal. This started a fashion for pressing seaweeds, and shops in some seaside resorts sold pressed seaweed pictures, usually with a verse as the centrepiece and the seaweeds arranged as a border. A very popular verse began 'Call us not weeds! We are flowers of the sea. . . .' Chapter 3 tells you how to prepare seaweed and make your own pictures with it.

Even more surprisingly, the Victorians and Edwardians used onion skin and skeleton leaves to produce pictorial effects, thus making natural collages which were sometimes very pretty but sometimes extremely ugly! A collage is a design made up of several different materials: for instance, pressed flowers, pieces of lichen, seaweed and skeleton leaves.

In the late Victorian and the Edwardian periods every young lady tried her hand at making a dried flower picture to convey a message. In the middle of the nineteenth century American ladies introduced a 'language of flowers'; ivy denoted friendship, a tulip represented true love and so on! Young women of that era composed pressed flower pictures where every bloom had a meaning, but in their enthusiasm to put over a message they often made their pictures too crowded and fussy. Today we tend to aim for simplicity, and the most attractive flower picture is usually the one which is not overcrowded. You can see some of the early designs in museums and compare them with modern flower and leaf etc. collages. These are pictures which include flowers and leaves of different textures, perhaps even seed-heads or lichens as well, but which concentrate on line and an uncluttered lay-out.

Making a Herbarium

The oldest and most common use for preserved plant material is to form a herbarium. This is a collection of pressed flowers, leaves, ferns, and grasses, classified according to family and mounted in an album or on looseleaf cards. Some herbariums, such as the one at Kew Gardens, London, are world-famous and used extensively for research in botanical and scientific work, but a private herbarium can be a source of pleasure and interest for a lifetime.

To prepare flowers for a herbarium it is necessary to include the stem and also at least one leaf. Arrange flowers, stems and leaves as naturally as possible on a sheet of fairly thick white paper and be sure that all petals and leaves lie quite flat before pressure is put on them. Use a pointed camel-hair paintbrush to ease out any curls or creases in petals or leaves. Once the specimens are dried it is better to leave them on the same paper on which they have been pressed (provided that it is not stained in any way) and keep them in position by thin strips of gummed paper over tops and bottoms of stems. (See Chapter 3 for directions for pressing.)

The loose sheets should be covered with transparent film (not the sticky-backed sort) to preserve the specimens and they can be kept in a ring binder or bound together in album form. You can sew the sheets together with strong thread, like a book, and then either sew them into a stout cover made of thick paper or thin card, or slip them into a folder. These can be bought at a stationer's for about 20p to 50p, according to the quality of the folder. It is very important to name each specimen, and the scientific and popular name of each should be neatly written or lettered on the sheet which contains it. For instance, if you include the great periwinkle, you should also give its scientific name, *Vinca major*. If you do not know the scientific name of any flower or other plant you can look it up in your local library. The librarian will advise on suitable books to consult, and two which you will find particularly helpful are mentioned on p. 64.

2   *When to gather in your harvest. What to pick or grow*

When and where to gather plant material

Before you can start to preserve plant material you must, of course, gather in your harvest, and it is very important to do this at the right time; the success of the whole process of preserving depends on it.

April to September is the part of the year during which flowers and leaves are easily available, but some ferns, grasses and seed-heads can be collected well into autumn, or even early winter.

The most important thing is to choose a dry day for picking any plant material. Anything picked when it is damp will soon become mildewed when it is pressed, and items hung up to dry will grow mouldy instead. The morning dew is just as dampening as rain, so wait for it to dry and aim to gather your harvest about midday. If you leave it until afternoon the sun on a summer's day may have had a burning effect and flowers will be past their prime.

It is better to cut flowers when they are just opening than to wait until they are in full bloom. The only exception to this is in gathering rose petals for pot pourri; then a full-blown rose with undamaged petals will suit your purpose.

Delphiniums are very popular as material for preserving, since the florets hold their colour well, whether pressed or dried by hanging. But try to cut them before the buds at the top open. The same applies to other spikes of flowers such as gladiolus or golden rod.

The greatest care needs to be exercised when harvesting such things as pampas grass and bulrushes. Both must be cut before they are fully ripe; bulrushes work best if gathered before they have developed their rich brown velvety texture, and pampas grass before it has become feathery. On the other hand, seed-heads are better left to dry right out on the plant, although if they are nearly ripe and bad weather seems imminent it is wiser to cut them and dry them off indoors than let them be spoilt by heavy rain or beaten down in a gale.

If you have a garden it will provide you with plenty of plant material, but you can also gather wild flowers, grasses, ferns, seed-heads and some types of fungi. They may come from hedgerows, fields, moorland, cliffs, woods, the banks of rivers and streams, or even the crevices of old walls. Wild flowers and plants give pleasure to everyone, so never take too much. In picking flowers select just one or two from a single plant and pick only as many as you need; never gather huge bunches which you know you will not be able to use, and *never* dig up or mutilate plants.

You may find some material in public parks or gardens, but certain rules must be observed. You may gather leaves or seeds which have fallen from trees, but the picking of anything at all from plants, shrubs or trees is strictly forbidden and is a punishable offence. In some public gardens a warden or park keeper may give you permission to take fallen flower-heads or petals, but this is not always the case and permission must be asked first.

Of course, one must never pick anything from a private garden without having asked permission and sometimes, in places such as nature reserves, it is forbidden to pick any wild flowers at all, so any notices to that effect should be carefully read and obeyed.

Plant material for pressing and drying

GARDEN FLOWERS

There are a number of plants which you can grow to provide you with material for pressing and drying. Pansies are among the most successful flowers; they press well, keep their colour and are easy to cultivate in the garden. Golden rod comes up year after year and dries well. Honesty is very useful for its silvery seed pods, which are revealed when the brown outer covers are gently rubbed away by thumb and first finger. It is a slightly untidy plant but, again, it is worth setting aside a corner in which it can grow.

Love-in-a-mist is a hardy annual which you can grow easily from seed and which should be left to seed, as its round, spiky seed-heads are most attractive and useful.

All the varieties of achillea (a member of the yarrow family) dry well and keep their colour, and the plants are hardy perennials (flowers which come up year after year).

The Cape Gooseberry (or Chinese Lantern) is famous for its bright orange seed-heads and once established in a garden it will spread rapidly.

Lavender is good for drying, and primroses, polyanthus and stachys (Lamb's Ear or Donkey's Ear) are all good for pressing, stachys for the lovely velvety leaves.

Some of the most useful plants to grow are helichrysum or everlasting flowers, also known as straw daisies. These come in a variety of bright colours and can be grown from seed in the garden or in boxes, tubs or pots. Statice is another good 'everlasting' flower to grow, as it dries well by hanging and keeps its colour for years; there are varieties in many colours.

Two less known 'everlasting' flowers are rhodanthe and xeranthemum, which produce pretty flowers in pastel shades of pink, mauve and white and keep their colour well when dried; they are not difficult to grow.

These are just a few suggestions. Many other flowers and leaves preserve well and you will soon discover the ones you would specially like to grow for yourself.

WILD FLOWERS

Picking wild flowers for preserving is often a matter of trial and error; some will do better than others. In theory practically anything can be preserved, but some flowers are tricky.

Buttercups come on the list of successful pressers, as they hold their colour. Vetch is another common wild flower which is usually successful although it presses to a delicate cream colour; wild violets are also good for pressing and keep their colour fairly well. These wild flowers, being smaller and more delicate than many of the garden flowers, need very careful handling when pressing but amply repay the time taken over them.

All types of heather are good for pressing but need a fairly heavy weight, as the stems are woody.

Cow parsley and the dainty lady's bedstraw are invaluable for pressed flower pictures and grow in most hedgerows.

When you are choosing flowers for pressing a good deal depends on the purpose for which you intend to use them. For instance, a flower which would have to be included in a herbarium may not be colourful or attractive enough for a flower picture, and a flower which presses may not dry successfully and will therefore not be suitable for use in a flower arrangement.

OTHER WILD PLANT MATERIAL

Ferns and grasses all press well, as do the leaves of many wild plants. Blackberry leaves turn to lovely colours late in their season, but they are prickly, so be careful when gathering them. Ivy leaves press well and are also found in pretty colours – the Victorians were always seeking what they called variegated ivy for their flower pictures.

Do not overlook seed-heads. You can gather long trails of old man's beard (wild clematis) for preserving in a glycerine solution (as explained in Chapter 3) and seed-heads of dock can be preserved in a similar way, while beech leaves are the most popular subject for that treatment. Beech leaves also press well.

FUNGI

For collages and flower arrangements some types of fungi may be gathered. The 'bracket' or 'ear' types which grow out of the trunks of old trees are the most satisfactory, provided the specimens are in good condition when they are picked and are not beginning to rot away or be eaten away by insects or slugs. This type of fungus will dry well.

3 How to preserve plant material

Pressing

By far the most widely used method of preserving flowers, leaves, grasses and ferns is pressing. It is possible to buy flower presses in craft shops and craft departments of some stores, and these range in price from about £1 to £5 or more, according to size and quality. But a home-made press will cost practically nothing and is quite as effective (even if not quite as elegant!) as a press bought in a shop.

    To make a press you will need two pieces of stout board (plywood is hardly thick enough), some sheets of clean blotting paper, a few old building bricks and a sheet of strong brown paper. The two pieces of board can be what size you like: 12 in. × 12 in. (approx. 30·5 cm. × 30·5 cm.) is quite a useful size but you can use larger or smaller pieces if you wish. The boards form the top and bottom of the press and folded sheets of blotting paper go between them like a sandwich. Even pressure must be applied at the top. Wrap each brick in strong brown paper and seal the ends with adhesive tape; this will prevent any brick dust from getting into the press. Then just lay the bricks on top of the press and you are all ready to start preparing flowers etc. to go into it.

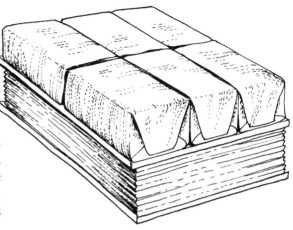

1 · *A home-made flower press*

If you learn carpentry at school, you will be able to make a more elaborate press. Bore holes in the two pieces of board and insert long screws to which wing nuts are attached at the top. The nuts can then be screwed down to the required pressure as the press is filled. Most shop-bought presses operate on this principle.

Special botanical paper can be bought and used instead of blotting paper, but if you want to be really economical you can use clean newspaper, although not being so absorbent as blotting paper it does not always give such good results. It is not advisable to press plant material in books; it often stains the pages and strains the binding.

Remember all items *must* be dry before they are put in the press and for best results press them as soon as possible after picking. This applies to both garden and wild material. To press, place the plant face downwards on a sheet of blotting paper and make sure that all the petals and leaves are flat. Any creases may be smoothed out with a clean, fine paintbrush. Pressure from thumb or first finger on the centre (the corolla) of a flower may be necessary to flatten it before it goes into the press. If a flower has a very hard or fat middle, take the petals off and press them separately; you will be able to reassemble them when they are pressed. To press the hard middle cut a hole in a piece of thick cardboard, just big enough to slip over the hard centre of the flower, so that it is level with the surface of the cardboard. Then press in the usual way. Incidentally, you may have to improvise centres for some flowers and this gives good scope for being both creative and ingenious!

For example, you could use a pressed marigold centre with poppy petals, because the centres of poppies are very difficult to press and have to be hung to dry to preserve them. It is up to you to decide how you can best show off both petals and centres to advantage, even if it means using a different centre from the one which the flower originally had.

Once having put the material satisfactorily into the press, place the bricks on top or tighten the wing nuts and then put the press in a place where it will not have to be disturbed for at least six weeks. Some thick leaves or petals may take up to twelve weeks to dry out completely; do not be tempted to take them out until they *are* quite dry. Keep the press in a dry but airy place: never put it in an airing cupboard or any other place where drying out will be too quick.

Using desiccants

Some flowers such as daffodils or thick-centred Shasta daisies will be extremely difficult, perhaps impossible, to press as they are, and for them you can use the dry sand method. There are in fact three substances which can be used for this method of drying: sand, borax and silica gel.

Sand means builders' or 'silver' sand and it must be absolutely clean and dry before use. Wash it in cold water, draining off the water several times until it is quite clear, then spread the sand on a shallow baking tray or something similar and put it in a warm oven until there is no moisture at all left in it.

Borax is cheaper than silica gel, especially if you use household borax (which can be obtained from hardware shops or the hardware departments of multiple stores) rather than the more refined type which is bought at the chemist's. Borax can be obtained pre-packed or, in some shops, weighed out to your requirements. Silica gel comes in crystal form and before it is used in drying flowers the crystals must be crushed to powder.

These materials are called desiccants, which means they absorb moisture, and to dry flowers in them you will need a container which has a tight-fitting (ideally an airtight) lid. A biscuit tin, a polythene cake-box, a lunch-box or something similar is ideal for the purpose, but a thick cardboard box can be used provided the lid fits really tightly. Flowers dried in this way need to have their stems cut very short in most cases.

Whether you use sand, borax or silica gel the technique is the same. Into the clean, dry container pour enough desiccant to cover the bottom to a depth of about two inches. For a flower such as a marigold push the stem into the powder until the flower-head is resting lightly on the top of the powder layer and then, very gently and very slowly, pour on more desiccant until the flower-head is completely buried. Make sure that the drying material goes between each petal and any leaves; a soft paintbrush is handy for this. Several flowers can be dried at the same time in the same container, but be sure that they do not touch each other. The flower-head should be buried to a depth of at least one inch in desiccant, with no part of it showing. Put on the lid, secure it firmly, and without shaking the box at all move it to a spot where it is not to be touched.

The time taken for drying in a desiccant ranges from one to six days, according to the type of flower. The time may be longer in very damp weather, so keeping the box in a warm, dry room speeds the drying process. To see if a flower is ready, gently brush the surface powder away with a paintbrush and lift the flower out very carefully, shaking it lightly to remove the drying material. The flower petals should be crisp and dry. If the flower is not ready put it back as before and leave for another twenty-four hours before examining it again.

Some of the popular flowers which dry successfully by this method include lilac (which takes about 2–3 days), marigolds (4–5 days, maybe a little longer for really big French marigolds), carnations (4–5 days), daffodils and narcissi (2–3 days), zinnias (3–4 days), camellias (4–5 days), roses (2–3 days, dry when buds are half open), begonia (3–4 days), thrift (2–3 days) and bluebells (2–3 days). But never be afraid to experiment, try many different species of flowers. You may also find that drying time varies; it all depends on the atmosphere and temperature of the room in which you keep the drying box.

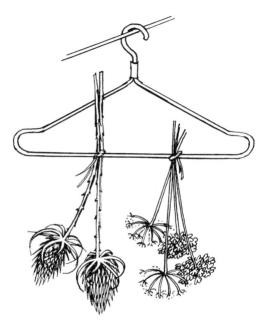

2 · *A simple way to dry flowers and seed-heads; tie them to a wire coat hanger.*

Drying naturally

The third method of drying flowers is very simple – it is just to hang them up, head downwards, in a dry, airy but dark room and allow them to dry naturally. The quicker the flowers dry the better they retain their colour, so warm air and darkness are necessary for best results. This is where an airing cupboard can be useful – if there is room and you are allowed to hang things to dry in it! Larkspur and delphiniums both do best if dried quickly in very warm dry atmosphere and *in the dark*, so the airing cupboard is ideal in that case. All the so-called everlasting flowers (mentioned in Chapter 2) should be dried by the hanging method and should be cut just as the flowers are opening. Tie flowers in bunches; it is a good idea to use a slip knot, as this will allow you to tighten the tie as the stems shrink in the drying process. To make a slip knot put the string under the bunch of flowers, leaving a fairly long piece on the right-hand side. Bring the two ends up, hold the left-hand one tightly and loop the right-hand one round it. Pass the right-hand end through the loop and pull it tight. The diagrams will show you how to do it (see fig. 3).

Some flowers will dry successfully by standing upright in any clean container. Tie in bunches but do not try to cram too many stems into each container; there must be a free flow of air around the flower-heads. Achillea is one of the most popular garden flowers for drying either by hanging or standing upright and the wild yarrow (a member of the same family) is also successfully

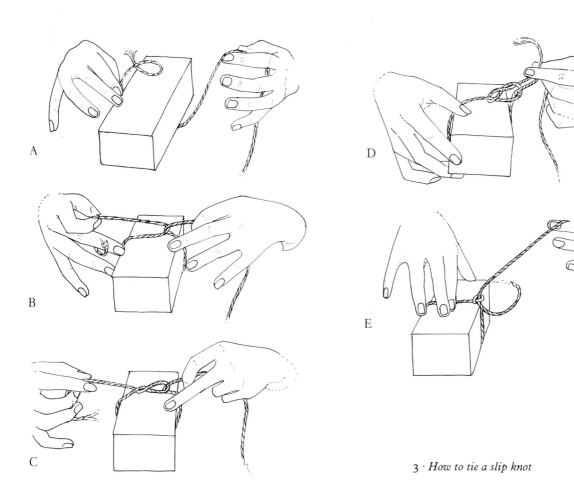

A

B

C

D

E

3 · *How to tie a slip knot*

dried by this method. One of the flower arranger's favourites is Bells of Ireland (Moluccella) which has spikes of lime-green bells. When dried by the hanging method the bells turn a rich cream colour. Bulrushes will dry by either the hanging or standing methods but if picked too ripe (and it is often difficult to gauge if they are in that condition when you pick them) have a nasty habit of bursting quite suddenly and showering fluffy seeds everywhere. You can guard against this to a certain extent by spraying them with hair lacquer after you have dried them.

Seed-heads which dry well if hung up are Chinese Lantern, poppy, love-in-a-mist, iris, and from the hedgerows dock, foxglove, teasel and wild clematis or old man's beard.

Glycerining

There is one other method of preserving leaves which you will certainly want to use if you are preserving material for flower arranging. The method is known as glycerining. In recent years some people have used motor-car anti-freeze solution instead of glycerine, but glycerine gives the most consistently satisfactory results, although it is more expensive. It is bought at a chemist's.

For this method you will need a glass jar, such as a jam jar or an old jug or any such receptacle which will withstand hot water. To prepare leaves and berries remove any which are damaged, and for leaves choose shapely sprays. With woody stems such as beech, split the end of the stem for about two inches (about five centimetres), to allow it to soak up the solution more easily. The quantity of solution you mix depends upon how much plant material you wish to treat at one time, but the quantities are always one part glycerine to two parts boiling water. The solution should come about two inches (five centimetres) up the jar or other receptacle, no matter how many stems you put into it; it is advisable to treat only a few stems at a time. Pour the glycerine into the jar, add the boiling water, and mix them thoroughly by shaking or stirring. Then just stand the sprays of leaves and/or berries in the solution and leave until the foliage has turned a soft brown and the berries have become lighter.

The time this takes to happen will vary considerably. Sprays with tough, woody stems such as beech usually take two to three weeks to soak up the glycerine mixture, although this varies with the age of the leaves; young beech leaves do not take as long as mature ones. Leathery leaves such as laurel and camellia or magnolia may take as long as a month, while ivy may have soaked its fill in a week. The longer leaves are left in the solution the darker they will get, but do not leave them too long or they will absorb too much solution, will become damp and eventually turn mouldy. It is advisable to check plant material in glycerine every few days, as it must be taken out before the solution starts oozing through the leaves. If you do see that happening, take the leaves out, dry the stems and pat the leaves dry between the folds of a soft cloth; then put them somewhere airy to dry out.

Material which has been glycerined can be stored in a box in a dry place and any solution left over can be kept in a screw-top jar and used again when reheated. Never store glycerined material in a plastic bag; it will go mouldy unless the air can get to it.

Beech is the favourite material for glycerining; the leaves turn different shades of brown according to their age. So if you glycerine sprays of young leaves in May or June they will be a light tan colour, in late July they will turn to a darker brown and leaves picked at the end of the summer, before they take their autumn tints, will be a really dark brown. It is advisable to glycerine some beech leaves at each of these stages, as they contrast charmingly in flower arrangements.

Other leaves which take the glycerine solution well are laurel, oak, holly (takes a long time to drink up the solution and turn colour), fatsia (big, leathery leaves which are most suitable material to place low down in a flower arrangement), eucalyptus and privet. The once popular foliage house plant aspidistra is an ideal subject for glycerining; the long leaves turn a lovely golden brown colour but must be watched carefully and removed from the glycerine as soon as they are coloured, otherwise they soak up too much and become spoilt.

As with other forms of plant preservation, glycerining is a matter of trial and error. Never hesitate to experiment. Some leaves will be very successful, others will not work at all, but that way you will learn and you may succeed in getting results with leaves which other people have not thought of trying to preserve. Types which do not take kindly to glycerining are the many varieties of cupressus, fir, larch and other trees with needle-like leaves. Thick, fleshy leaves such as those of cacti and succulents are not suitable either.

Pressing seaweed

We have seen how Queen Victoria as a young girl prepared an album of pressed seaweeds and how this started a fashion for seaweed pictures. Seaweed albums are not often made now, and modern seaweed pictures often include other material such as lichen and any plant material which teams suitably with it. However, two ladies recently staged an exhibition in Cornwall and had fifty framed pictures on show, all of them consisting of seaweed arranged in abstract patterns. If you find seaweeds interesting you may well like to start a collection of pressed specimens, just as children and adults did in the last century and as museums do today.

Seaweed is pressed in much the same way as flowers, although there is a little more work to be done on it first.

Once collected from the sea or shore the seaweed must be attended to as soon as possible after you get home. You will need a shallow dish, some unglazed white paper, some clean blotting paper and some butter muslin or similar material. You will also need some sea salt, and this can be bought in packets from health food stores or chemists. The salt is to be added to the water in which you wash the seaweed and is very important; without it you will not get results. Never try to make do by using ordinary table or cooking salt, as this will spoil your specimens, discolouring the seaweed and making some of it sticky and nasty.

First of all make up the salt water by dissolving one and a half ounces of salt in every quart of fresh water you use. Then cut a piece of paper slightly larger than the specimen to be pressed and submerge the paper in the dish of salt water, disturbing the water as little as possible. Allow the water to settle, and when it is quite still *float* the piece of seaweed on the paper and arrange it with a soft paintbrush. Lift the paper and seaweed very carefully from the water and lay them on a piece of blotting paper; cover the seaweed very gently with a piece of muslin (already cut to size) and then put another piece of blotting paper on top of that.

Build up your pile of seaweed specimens this way, then put the pile between two boards and apply light pressure: a book such as a telephone directory is suitable. The blotting paper may need changing after a few days and when the seaweed is quite dry take the specimens from the press, peeling the muslin off very carefully. It is wise not to remove the muslin until you are actually going to do something with a piece of seaweed; once pressed and dried it is very fragile and will not stand a lot of handling. So if you are going to make a seaweed picture get everything else ready beforehand. The seaweed has then only to be placed in the position in which you wish it to remain. Instructions are given in Chapter 5.

If you do not want to use seaweed for making pictures you can mount your specimens in an album, as with a collection of pressed flowers, or you can mount each specimen on a loose card, cover it with cellophane paper and keep your collection with the cards standing upright in a lidded box such as a shoe box.

Preserving fungi

Fungi are preserved by drying and the best way is to put them somewhere where they will dry slowly and not in an intense heat. Lay the pieces on a thick newspaper and put that on an old tray or a piece of stout cardboard; take care to see that the pieces of fungus do not touch each other. They must then be left undisturbed to dry. If you have room on a high shelf in the kitchen or other warm room that is ideal; just place the tray on the shelf and leave it. Or if there is room in the airing cupboard that, too, is a suitable place. Look at the fungi from time to time, as in drying out some of the moisture will be transferred to the newspaper and so it will be necessary to change the paper occasionally. Large bracket fungus will take several months to dry out completely, but when it is dry it is light to handle and becomes quite hard. When it is quite dry store it in a box with a closely fitting lid and in which you have previously sprinkled some insecticide powder: this prevents insects from eating into the fungi. Check it from time to time to ensure that it is still in good condition. There may have been insects in it which you did not notice or which were not visible to the naked eye, and after a while they may become active again. If you do notice that a piece of fungus is being eaten away by insects or going powdery, throw it away at once. It will only infect the other pieces if you leave it in the box and there is no way you can stop the rot.

Preserving cones

Before storing away cones brush them with an old toothbrush (for big ones use a stiff nailbrush or small scrubbing brush, but do not make them damp) and dust them all over with an insecticide powder. They are best stored in a box with an airtight lid.

4 How to make Pot Pourri

One way of keeping summer fragrance in your home all the year round is to make pot pourri. As we saw in Chapter 1, this is a very old art and still as popular today as it was in times gone by. Things filled with pot pourri make delightful Christmas and birthday gifts as well as being pleasant to make for yourself.

There are many different recipes for making pot pourri, some using expensive essences but many being simple and inexpensive to prepare from ingredients which are readily available. Many are classic recipes which have not changed at all over the years.

Pot pourri is made from sweetly scented flower petals, aromatic leaves such as lemon plant, geranium or mint, and sometimes whole small scented flowers. The rules for picking are the same as those given in Chapter 2 for picking flowers and leaves for pressing.

You can vary the types of flowers and leaves you use, making different combinations to create your own scents; pot pourri certainly need not be confined to rose petals, as many people think.

Petals only are used from large flowers; small flower-heads can be used whole; leaves must be stripped from stalks. Having gathered your material, spread it out on a newspaper or old sack and put it in the sun to dry. Needless to say, do not do this on a windy day! Keep each variety separate. A good way to do this is to spread petals, leaves and flowers on shallow trays; the lids of biscuit tins or boot and shoe boxes are very suitable. The material takes several days to dry properly, so watch the weather and take in your trays at the first sign of any moisture in the air, and always take them indoors before nightfall, not putting them out again until mid-morning. Occasionally shake them gently so that all the material dries evenly. If the weather turns dull or damp the material can be dried in an airing cupboard, although you must watch it carefully and see that it does not literally burn. It should be taken from the cupboard when it reaches a stage of crispness like thin melba toast or fairly stiff paper.

For pot pourri never dry petals, flowers or leaves in front of a coal, electric, or gas fire, or on a stove or heater. Not only is this dangerous if you have the material on paper or cardboard trays, it also dries out the moisture too quickly from the petals and so destroys the fragrance. No artificial additive ever quite replaces the natural scent.

Once the material is quite dry you are ready to start mixing your pot pourri. The quantity you make varies, of course, according to the amount you put into it. Perhaps in starting you would like to make only a small quantity of each fragrance and see how you get on. You can always double or treble the quantities when you achieve a mixture which you particularly like.

Rose pot pourri is a very old favourite. Try to choose petals from roses which have a fairly strong scent: some of the modern hybrid strains have very little scent, having been bred for colour and appearance rather than perfume. Although the spice which you will add will draw out what scent there is in the petals, it is always better if they have their own fairly pronounced scent in the first place.

Rose pot pourri

For rose pot pourri you will need two teacupfuls of dried rose petals and one teacupful of the dried petals of syringa or mock orange (Philadelphus). Mix them together by gently stirring with your fingers or a small plastic spoon and then add one ounce (25 g) of powdered orris root (obtainable from a chemist), one ounce (25 g) of ground coriander seeds and one large teaspoonful of ground cinnamon. Mix all the added ingredients together with the petals, using a plastic spoon, and put the mixture into a plastic bag, closing the bag securely with a rubber band or wire tie to keep the air out. For the next three weeks keep the bag tightly closed but gently shake it at fairly regular intervals, to move the mixture about.

At the end of three weeks you can open up the bag and decant the pot pourri into a pretty container such as a jar, bowl or bottle; or you can use it to fill little sachets to keep in drawers with clothes or bed linen, or in little bags to hang in the wardrobe. If you are using jars which have contained bath salts, or bottles which have had bath oil in them, be sure to wash and dry them thoroughly before putting pot pourri into them, in order to avoid conflicting scents. Orris root powder (made from the root of an iris) is very important in making pot pourri: it acts as a fixative to hold the scent, so never try doing without it. The result will be disappointing, as the scent will soon fade from the pot pourri.

Geranium leaf pot pourri

Instead of roses try a mixture of scented geranium leaves gently crushed in the hand when the leaves are dry. One cup of crushed leaves combined with one teaspoonful of ground allspice, half a teaspoonful of grated nutmeg and half an ounce (12·5 g) of powdered orris root makes a beautiful musky pot pourri with quite an exotic scent of the East.

Sachets

Small quantities of dried leaves and petals can be used to make miniature sachets for a box which contains writing paper. Use muslin for the sachet and sew it neatly into flat envelope shape, fill with dried petals and leaves and seal the flap of the envelope with firm stitching. Fill the envelope well but do not let it bulge and become a pillow.

One simple fragrance for this purpose has a scent in which mint predominates and is particularly pleasing for writing paper. The

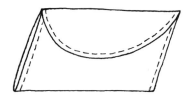

.4 · *Two shapes for lavender sachets – one made from a long strip of muslin sewn up each side, the other made in an evelope shape. In both designs sew where dotted lines are shown.*

following amounts make enough to fill one sachet: one tablespoonful mint leaves, one tablespoonful lemon verbena, one tablespoonful lemon balm, one tablespoonful of rosebuds. Dry the ingredients, then crumble them lightly between the fingers and mix
them well together with the fingers or a plastic spoon. Fill the
sachet with the mixture and stitch it down at once. Lavender,
thyme and lemon balm make another pleasant combination.

Muslin bags

Muslin bags filled with aromatic herbs will help to keep moths
away from wardrobes and drawers. Mixtures of equal quantities of
cloves, lavender, cinnamon, nutmeg, thyme and mint act as
deterrents in this way. Such things as cloves, nutmegs and seeds
must be ground to powder before being bagged in muslin, and
leaves must be crumbled after drying. If you want to give the bags
as presents, decorate them with ribbon. A set of three or six, each
with a different mixture or all the same (according to how much of
each ingredient you have), arranged in a box and tied with a ribbon
bow into which a small dried flower posy has been tucked, makes a
very acceptable gift for all occasions.

Pressed flowers and pot pourri

Recently at an exhibition in Belgium I saw a charming idea for
combining pressed flowers and pot pourri. A plain wine glass had

5 · *Two shapes for lavender bags –
a well-filled round one and a lightly-filled
longer one. The round one does not need
stitching, just tying tightly at the
top; the longer one is stitched up
both sides.*

been lined with pressed pansies, which were attached to the glass, faces outward, with touches of a colourless adhesive such as Copydex or Pritt. (This is in the form of a solid stick, very clean to use and obtainable from all good stationers.) The glass was then filled with pot pourri and 'stoppered' with a circle of cork about $\frac{1}{4}''$ thick and fitting tightly into the glass.

Experiment with your own pot pourri mixtures and do not hesitate to try something out of the ordinary. If you invent a totally new recipe for pot pourri keep it as your own secret and do not divulge it to your friends. The Victorians liked to invent their own recipes, which produced much excitement among friends who were all making their own pot pourri.

5 *Things to make*

Gifts of anything to do with flowers are always welcome and there are many things you can make from the plant material which you have preserved. So start planning now for birthdays and Christmas, and also make some pretty things for yourself.

Presents made with pressed flowers

GIFT TAGS

First, pressed flowers. As with every craft, it is best to start with something simple; you will soon develop the knack of working with pressed material and then you can go on to more complicated designs. Gift tags are a good choice for the beginner. You will need some thin card (white or coloured), adhesive (Copydex or Pritt) and two fine paintbrushes. Cut the card to size and choose the flowers or leaves you want to use. Arrange them attractively on the card and keep the design uncluttered. Use one of the paintbrushes to move them about; the less dried material is handled the better it is for it.

When all is arranged to your satisfaction use the other paintbrush to apply a tiny dab of adhesive to the back of each flower etc. (or you may prefer to dab it on from a Pritt stick) and apply light pressure with the forefinger to ensure that each flower etc. is firmly attached to the card. Beware of using too much adhesive; it can ruin the whole thing. The merest dab is quite enough. Leave the card to dry between the folds of a sheet of clean paper and with light pressure (such as a book) on top. When the adhesive is dry, cover the design with a transparent adhesive film. W. H. Smith Self Adhesive Covering Film, Fablon and Transpaseal are all good for the purpose, and all are obtainable in rolls from about 25 p. Cut a piece of film the exact size of the tag, peel off the backing paper and place the sticky side over the design, smoothing gently to make sure it is properly stuck. Punch a small hole in the top left-hand corner of the tag and thread through a piece of thin string or embroidery cotton, for attaching it to the gift.

CARDS

Cards for Christmas, birthdays and other occasions can be made in the same way. If you are good at lettering you can put some words such as 'Best Wishes' on the card before signing it, or for a professional-looking finish use 'rub on' lettering. Small packs or single sheets of letters are obtainable at stationers' shops from about 30p. Instructions come with the packs and are very simple; the letters are just placed over the card and rubbed with a blunt instrument such as a lolly stick. You can add a further nice touch by decorating the card with a ribbon bow.

CALENDARS

Calendars can be made in the same way as greetings cards, but bind the edges with coloured Sellotape and attach a loop for hanging, plus, of course, the calendar tab! Tabs can be bought at most stationers' from about October onwards for the coming year; they range in price from about 3p to 10p each, according to size, and are attached to the calendar with two pieces of ribbon to match the hanging loop.

TABLE MATS

Pressed leaves (especially those which have retained autumn colouring) make attractive table mats. For mats you will need some glass or stout perspex, cut to size. A useful size is 6 in. × 6 in. (15·5 cm. × 15·5 cm.) If you are using glass ask for 24 oz. or 32 oz. (600 g or 800 g) thickness, as this will withstand having hot dishes put on it. Many hardware shops will cut glass to size at little or no extra cost. You will also need some thin card, some really strong thick (not corrugated) cardboard and some pieces of felt for backing the mats to prevent them from slipping on or scratching the table. Leaves can be arranged either naturally or in a geometric pattern. First cut the paper (or thin card) and cardboard to size and stick the paper on to the cardboard. Now arrange the design, in the same way as for greetings cards. Leave to dry. When it is quite dry place a piece of glass or perspex (clean and free from all finger marks!) over the design and bind the edges neatly with adhesive tape such as Sellotape X, which comes in several colours. Then back the mat with felt, using an adhesive to make it stick. Small coasters for glasses can be made in the same way.

FINGER PLATES FOR DOORS

An unusual use for pressed flowers and leaves is decorating finger plates for doors. For these you will need to create long, narrow designs, so try to use plants with long stalks in your design to give it flow and movement. Transparent finger plates, complete with screws for fixing, can be bought in most hardware shops. Mount the plant material on card (as for table mats) and cut to the size of the finger plate. Fasten the card to the plate with just the tiniest dab of adhesive in each corner and then screw the plate to the door.

PRESSED FLOWER PICTURES

Pressed flower pictures can also be tackled when you have become proficient. The design is built up in exactly the same way as for a greetings card but it will, of course, be far more elaborate and there is scope for using a greater variety of pressed material. Points to remember in designing a pressed flower picture are not to overcrowd it, not to have too many straight lines, to vary shapes and sizes as much as you can and to avoid crossed stems whenever possible. One word of warning: never hang a flower picture in direct sunlight, it will quickly fade.

Having made your picture you will want to frame it. You can either use a ready-made frame bought in a shop (or perhaps you already have one at home) or cover the picture with glass or perspex and bind the edges in the same way as for table mats. It is very important that the flowers be in direct contact with the glass, otherwise they will curl, so do not put the picture behind a mount before you frame it. If you want to hang it up you can buy hanging rings from a picture-framing shop and attach them to the back.

6 · *In this pressed flower picture the daisy-like flowers were built up from pink and white dahlia petals. The leaves included Virginia creeper and variegated geranium. The framing was done very simply with insulating tape or passe partout holding the glass down tightly.*

(Picture by Mrs Mary Cole)

7 · Pressed flower picture :
   florets of lady's bedstraw encircle
   a design of pressed sorrel and campion flowers
   on a pressed ivy leaf – on black card.
   (Picture by Mrs Mary Cole)

Presents made with preserved flowers

MINIATURE FLOWER PICTURES

Now we turn to preserved flowers etc. and there are numerous possibilities for making things with them. Many needlework shops sell brooch frames which are intended to take small embroidery pictures, but they will also take a miniature preserved flower picture. Use the smallest of your dried material, nipping off a single floret or even single petals, perhaps cutting out miniature leaf shapes from larger leaves and taking single feathery seeds from a whole seed-head of something like wild clematis. You then arrange these on paper already cut to size to fit the brooch frame, stick them down with a tiny touch of adhesive, as for pressed flower

8 · *Dried flowers in a brooch*

designs, and then fit the whole thing into the brooch frame. The picture is fastened very simply into the frame by pressing down four tiny tabs attached to the frame at the back.

Another idea for using preserved material is to create a miniature picture in a curtain ring. For this you will need a large wooden or plastic curtain ring and a piece of cartridge paper or thin card. Cut the paper to the exact size of the ring and again build up your design; tiny buds of the 'everlasting flowers', single florets of brightly coloured statice, small bracken leaves and so on are nicely in scale for this type of design. When all the plant material is firmly stuck put some stronger adhesive on the back of the ring and place it over the 'picture', pressing it down hard. Leave to dry and then attach a ready-to-stick-on hanging ring (obtainable in packets from stationers' shops) to the back.

An attractive picture can be made by using the lid of a plastic tub of the type in which margarine, ready-mixed salads etc. are sold. Wash the lid thoroughly and when it is dry spray or paint it all over with quick-drying enamel paint. When the paint is quite dry cut a scrap of fabric (preferably velvet but any unpatterned material can be used) to the exact size of the centre of the top of the lid and stick it on. When that is dry start doing your design. This is confined to the fabric in the centre of the lid; the raised edge of the lid makes a nice 'frame' for the picture. A half moon shape in dried flowers, leaves and seed-heads is very effective (see fig. 10) and a change from the more usual 'posy' design in the centre. In this shape of design the curve of the arrangement follows the curve of the 'frame'. When the flower-heads etc. are suitably arranged stick them down with the usual adhesive, and when they are firmly stuck you can attach a hanging ring at the back. A calendar tab attached with two strips of Sellotape or insulating tape makes this into a useful Christmas present.

9 · *Design in a curtain ring (made by Joyce Smith, aged 10)*

10 · *Arrangement in a carton top*

11 · *Paperweight*
(made by Marian Cooper, aged 12)

PAPERWEIGHTS

A novel idea for using pressed or dried flowers etc. is to mount them in a paperweight. Plain glass paperweights for this purpose may be bought at some needlework or craft shops, or by mail order (see list of suppliers, p. 63). The paperweight has the floral design mounted in much the same way as table mats are made. Place the paperweight on a piece of thick cardboard and mark around it, so that the base will be the exact size. Do your design on the card, and when it is dry run a thin line of strong adhesive (such as Uhu) around the edge of the card, put the paperweight on it and press down firmly. When the adhesive has dried, cover the base of the paperweight with Contact 'baize', which is self-adhesive and obtainable from most good stationers.

FLOWER BALLS

A pretty use for helichrysum flowers is to make flower balls. Such a ball is an unusual thing for a small bridesmaid to carry at a wedding, and a ball hung in a room (well away from fires or electric light fitments) makes a charming decoration. You will need a ball of Styrofoam (which can be bought at a florist's) and one yard of narrow ribbon. Thread the ribbon through the ball (see fig. 12a), using a knitting needle to make the hole; thread the ribbon through double, leaving a loop for hanging it and tying a small knot to prevent the ribbon from pulling back into the ball. Leave the two ends flowing.

There are two ways of covering the ball with flower-heads: you can either mount the heads on short wires (see Chapter 6 for instructions on wiring) and push them into the foam, as with a 'tree' (see p. 54), or you can stick the heads on instead of wiring them. If you are sticking them use strong adhesive. Uhu is a suitable brand; follow the instructions on the pack. Put a dab on the back of the flower-head and a dab on the foam ball, and as soon as the adhesive is tacky press the flower-head on to the ball. Cover the foam completely in this way and hang the ball up until the adhesive is quite dry. Then tie the ends of the ribbon into a bow close against the flowers (see fig. 12).

A   B

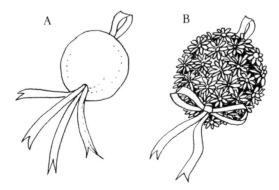

12a · *How to thread the ribbon through when making a flower ball*

12b · *A completed flower ball*

SEAWEED PICTURES

A seaweed picture is done in much the same way as a pressed flower picture and all the same rules apply, but to add interest and give a modern touch you can use dark grey paper and create a simple landscape 'painting'. Use white poster paint to draw some mountains and perhaps a few trees in the background and then place your pressed seaweed specimens so as to look like trees or plants growing in the foreground. Stick them down with Copydex or Pritt in the same way as pressed flowers. Or you can arrange them as the Victorians did, into dainty sprays, in the same way as making up spray designs of pressed flowers and leaves. Or you may like to copy another Victorian idea and use pressed seaweed as a border around a picture, such as a picture postcard, a print or a picture cut from a magazine. Sea views are, of course, particularly appropriate!

POMANDERS

Pomanders, much in use in Elizabethan times, have come back into fashion, but home-made ones often prove a disappontment because instead of lasting almost for ever (as a good pomander should) they rot or shrivel after a very short time. The secret is in the drying, so here is a way of making a pomander which should last for a very long time if you follow the directions faithfully.

You will need one orange, one ounce (25 g) of whole cloves and three tablespoonfuls of orris root powder, also a piece of muslin for

13 · Collage picture : this collage of natural dried materials is done on black paper.
A simple outline of mountains is painted at the back and the design uses
various pressed materials, e.g. a piece of thin root, coralline seaweed, moss,
tiny pieces of heather and small pressed flowers. (Picture by Mrs Nancy
Bowyer-Smith)

wrapping the pomander. The orange should be ripe but *not* over-ripe and not blemished or bruised. With a knitting needle make holes all over the orange, so close to each other that they almost touch but not so close that they develop into one big hole! Press one clove into each hole, pushing it in so that the head is against the orange skin. Put the orris root powder in a large basin or mixing bowl and roll the orange in it. Take the orange out and sift the powder over it until it is completely coated. Put it carefully into a brown paper bag (not allowing any more of the powder to rub off than you can help), twist the bag shut and put it away in a dark, dry but not hot cupboard to ripen. This may take three or four weeks.

At the end of that time take the orange from the bag, wrap it in muslin without allowing too much of the powder to rub off, and then wrap it in a square of dainty, thin material, bunching the ends at the top and tying with a ribbon. In time it will become completely dry and hard like a stone. You can then remove the muslin and other material wrapping, and hang it in a wardrobe or cupboard or as a decoration in a room. You can even carry it like a handbag and have a pleasant aroma always surrounding you! Incidentally, Cardinal Wolsey was said to have always worn a pomander attached to his girdle when he was going out, as it helped to disguise the unpleasant smells of the streets in those days, and as it swung the scent wafted up to him.

6 *Flower arrangements*

Preserved plant material is ideal for flower arrangements. These are particularly useful in winter, when fresh flowers are scarce and expensive and a dried arrangement can be a little bit of summer lingering in your home on the dark winter days.

The basic requirements for flower arrangement are a pair of scissors (preferably but not necessarily flower scissors), a variety of containers (just about anything from a plain soup plate to an elaborate vase!), some stub wires (obtainable from florists and some garden shops) and some plastic foam material such as Oasis or Styrofoam (also obtainable at florists' and some garden shops). The foam material comes in rectangular blocks, balls, cones or cylinders, all priced from about 25 p according to size. It can easily be cut to size with a sharp knife.

To start a dried arrangement select a container and a piece of foam material of the size and shape desired. If the container is not too shallow fill the bottom with some clean sand before inserting the foam material; this prevents the arrangement from falling over, as the dried or preserved flowers etc. are very light. If possible fit the foam tightly into the container; if it does not fit tightly secure it with rubber bands or thin string passed crosswise over it and beneath the container. The bands or string will later be hidden by the plant material.

The basic rule for flower arranging is to place large items low in the arrangement. Build up the outline of the design first, using the more delicate and pointed items of the plant material and then fill in with larger leaves and flowers, with one large flower or a close group of smaller flowers placed fairly low down in the centre as a focal point and the largest leaves and flowers placed really low in the arrangement. It is important that foam material and the fastening (known to flower arrangers as the mechanics of an arrangement) are hidden from view, and large preserved leaves or bracket and ear fungi can often be used to cover them. In a shallow dish pretty stones can be grouped to cover the foam material, as well as weighting down the container.

Making a seed pod tree

A seed pod 'tree' makes an unusual table decoration. For this you will need a cone of plastic foam, a piece of dowelling or garden cane and a small, clean flower pot. Push the stick right into the foam and cut it to the length required. This is the 'trunk' of the 'tree'. Plug any holes in the base of the flower pot and fill it with dry sand; embed the 'tree' in this. Suitable material for a 'tree' includes small fir cones, poppy seed-heads, beech masts, Chinese Lanterns and oak apples. Decide how you are going to make the pattern, either in vertical lines or in rings around the cone.

All that remains is to push the plant material into the foam. Anything with a stiff stem will go in easily; if there is any difficulty in getting it in make a small hole with a knitting needle, to take the stem. Fir cones and Chinese Lanterns will need to be wired and fig. 14 shows you how to do this. Push each cone etc. in as far as the stem will go, so that the foam is completely covered and there is none of it showing anywhere. For a Christmas table decoration you can spray the finished 'tree' with gold or silver paint, or you can push a few holly berries in between the dried material.

If you have been able to preserve any berries in glycerine, these team well with glycerined beech leaves and dried corn (wheat, barley or oats) to form a harvest type of arrangement in the winter.

15 · A 'tree' table decoration made of poppy seed-heads and Chinese Lanterns stuck into a cone of styrofoam mounted on a short stick

14 · How to add a stem to a cone by twisting wire round the lower scales

16 · *Spray on polystyrene – statice on a piece
   of ceiling tile
   (made by Jeremy Warner, aged 6)*

Small dried flower arrangements

Small dried flower arrangements are always popular on bazaar stalls, and can be done in containers which would otherwise be thrown away, such as yoghurt cartons, margarine tubs, detergent bottles cut down to three-quarter size, and plastic trays on which tomatoes etc. are sold. Make the containers attractive by spray-painting them in any colour or by covering them with wallpaper or pretty wrapping paper. Decorators' shops, builders' merchants or do-it-yourself shops may perhaps be able to give you an out-of-date wallpaper pattern book if you ask them and this is a real treasure trove for material to transform containers. Woodgrain pattern papers or some of the rough textured stone-patterned papers will make an ordinary plastic carton into something really special-looking!

You will almost surely want to use helichrysums in many of your flower arrangements, but although the flower-heads preserve well and are most colourful the stems shrivel and break and go limp. So the flower-heads must be mounted on wire. This is done by taking a florists' stub wire and bending over one end to form a tiny crook. Push the other end of the wire into the centre of the 'eye' of the flower-head and pull it through gently until the crook is hidden in the soft centre. This needs careful handling, as the crook must not be pulled right through the flower-head, so take your time over the operation. It is often better to insert the wires before the flower-head is completely dry, as that way it dries out on the wire and is

17 · *How to insert a stub wire in a flower-head. Pull it down gently so that the looped end of the wire is hidden in the centre of the flower head.*

not loose and wobbly. Incidentally, 20g. wire is the best gauge for mounting flower-heads. The smaller the flower the thinner must be the wire you will use. Most shops which stock such things have them in a choice of thicknesses. You can use wires in this way to make false stems on almost any flower.

Buttonholes and posies

Seed-heads and everlasting flowers make unusual buttonholes or little posies to tuck into a ribbon bow when a present has been gift-wrapped. In order to make them neat and not likely to prick fingers or clothes, the stems (whether natural or wires) must be bound and for this purpose you can buy reels of florists' self-adhesive tape in green or brown. Bind the tape tightly around the stems and snip off all the ends neatly.

Hollow-stemmed flowers such as daffodils which have been cut short and dried by the sand or borax method are very fragile when dry and will not stand having wires thrust into them. To lengthen them a wheaten straw can be pushed gently into the short hollow stem and a little dab of adhesive at its tip will ensure that it is firmly anchored.

Appendices

Some plants which are good for preserving
List of Suppliers
Books for reference

Some plants which are good for preserving

PRESSING

Garden flowers
Pansy (Viola)
Polyanthus
Rose petals

Wild flowers
Buttercup (Ranunculus)
Vetch (Leguminosae family)
Lady's bedstraw (*Galium verum*)
Cow parsley (Umbelliferae family)
Primrose (*Primula vulgaris*)

Leaves (Garden and/or wild)
Blackberry (bramble) (*Rubus fruticosus*)
Ivy (Hedera)
Common beech (*Fagus sylvatica*).
    Also Copper beech (*Fagus cuprea*)
Lamb's or donkey's ear (*Stachys lanata*)
Cotoneaster – all varieties when they
    turn red in autumn

DRYING

Garden flowers

Golden rod (Solidago)
Honesty (*Lunaria biennis*)
Yarrow family (Achillea)
Lavender (Lavandula)
Everlasting flower or straw daisy (Helichrysum)
Rhodanthe (Helipterum)
Xeranthemum
Bells of Ireland (Moluccella)
Delphinium – and also other members
    of the larkspur family

Wild flowers

Heather (Erica)
Yarrow (Achillea)

LEAVES AND SEED-HEADS

Garden plants

Poppy (Papaveraceae family)
Cape gooseberry or Chinese lantern (Physalis)
Iris (Iridaceae family)
Love-in-a-mist (*Nigella damascena*)
Honesty (*Lunaria biennis*)

Wild plants

Dock (Polygonaceae family)
Wild clematis (old man's beard or traveller's joy),
    (*Clematis vitalba*)
Wild teasel (*Dipsacus sylvestris*)
Great reed mace (generally known as bulrush)
    (*Typha latifolia*)

DRYING IN DESICCANTS
Garden flowers

Ox-eye daisy (*Chrysanthemum leucanthemum*).
    Also other members of Chrysanthemum family
Daffodil (Narcissus)
Lilac (*Syringa vulgaris*)
Marigold (Calendula)
Carnation (Dianthus)
Zinnia
Camellia (*Camellia japonica*)

GLYCERINING
Common beech (*Fagus sylvatica*) and
    Copper beech (*Fagus cuprea*)
Holly (*Ilex aquifolium*)
Laurel (Lauraceae family)

List of Suppliers

Flower presses. John Adam Toys from larger branches of W. H. Smith & Son Ltd, from £1.25 to £3.45.
  Habitat Flower Press from most large department stores, £1.75 and £2.75.
Perspex. Clear and coloured, cut to size. Abbey Products, The Old House, Chudleigh, Newton Abbot, Devon.
Paperweights. Harry Thorn & Son, China and Hardware, 119 Fore Street, Exeter, Devon. Send s.a.e. for details and price list.
Pot Pourri. Spices and herbs, most items for pot pourri, Culpeper Ltd, 21 Bruton Street, London W.1, or branches at 9 Flask Walk, Hampstead, London N.W.3, and 14 Bridewell Alley, Norwich, Norfolk. A catalogue, for ordering items by post, is obtainable from Culpeper Ltd, Hadstock Road, Linton, Cambridge.
Coarse sea salt for washing seaweed. Culpeper Ltd, addresses as above.
Herb plants and seeds, for growing for pot pourri. The Old Rectory Herb Garden, Rectory Lane, Ightham, Sevenoaks, Kent.

Prices and addresses correct at time of writing.

Books for reference

The Concise British Flora in Colour by W. Keble Martin, Ebury
    Press and Michael Joseph 1965.
The Oxford Book of Garden Flowers, by E. B. Anderson *et al.,*
    Oxford University Press 1963.